Searchlight BOOKS

Celebrating Failure

Great Engineering Fails

Barbara Krasner

Lerner Publications ◆ Minneapolis

On the cover: Destruction at an apartment building in East London, one day after a gas explosion in May 1968. The explosion caused an entire corner of the building to collapse.

Lerner Publications Company
An imprint of Lerner Publishing Group, Inc.
241 First Avenue North
Minneapolis, MN 55401 USA

For reading levels and more information, look up this title at www.lernerbooks.com.

Main body text set in Adrianna Regular.
Typeface provided by Chank.

Library of Congress Cataloging-in-Publication Data

Names: Krasner, Barbara, author.
Title: Great engineering fails / Barbara Krasner.
Description: Minneapolis : Lerner Publications, [2020] | Series: Searchlight books. Celebrating failure | Includes bibliographical references and index. | Audience: Ages 8–10. | Audience: Grades 4–6. | Summary: "No one will argue that engineering takes top talent, but what are the world's biggest engineering fails? Readers can find out all about them and discover how even fails can sometimes lead to engineering feats!"— Provided by publisher.
Identifiers: LCCN 2019016706 (print) | LCCN 2019981215 (ebook) | ISBN 9781541577343 (lb : alk. paper) | ISBN 9781541589285 (pb : alk. paper)
Subjects: LCSH: Engineering—Juvenile literature. | System failures (Engineering)—Juvenile literature.
Classification: LCC TA149 .K735 2020 (print) | LCC TA149 (ebook) | DDC 620/.00452—dc23

LC record available at https://lccn.loc.gov/2019016706
LC ebook record available at https://lccn.loc.gov/2019981215

Manufactured in the United States of America
1-46756-47747-6/18/2019

Contents

Chapter 1

FROM WRONG TO WRIGHT

Since ancient times, humans have dreamed of flying through the sky. In the eighteenth century, French scientists built the first hot-air balloons. In the early nineteenth century, a British inventor made the first glider, an aircraft without an engine. Other inventors tried to build airplanes, or flying machines with engines.

In November 1783, a hot-air balloon carried two Frenchmen into the skies above Paris. This was the first-ever human flight.

Many aircraft builders failed. Otto Lilienthal, a German engineer, crashed on a glider flight in 1896. He was badly injured and died the next day. American physicist Samuel Langley built an airplane with a gas engine. In the early twentieth century, the plane crashed twice in the Potomac River. So Langley gave up on airplanes.

Otto Lilienthal was the first person to successfully pilot a glider. But he died after a glider crash.

Sky's the Limit

Wilbur and Orville Wright didn't give up. They ran a bicycle business in Dayton, Ohio. They also built aircraft. In 1900, the brothers tested their first glider at Kitty Hawk, North Carolina. The glider flew, but not as high as the Wrights hoped it would. They came back to Kitty Hawk the next year with a new glider. It was hard to control.

The Wright brothers built gliders first and then learned to make airplanes.

As Wilbur Wright runs alongside, his brother Orville makes the first successful airplane flight on December 17, 1903.

The Wrights learned from their mistakes. They experimented with different wing designs. Finally, they built a glider that worked well. Then they added an engine and propellers to make an airplane. The Wrights made their first successful airplane flight in December 1903.

The Wrights kept building airplanes. Other aviators built them too. Soon people were using airplanes to carry mail, cargo, and passengers. The aviation industry was born.

The Wright brothers helped usher in the era of aviation. This photo of a Boeing 40 was taken in May 1938.

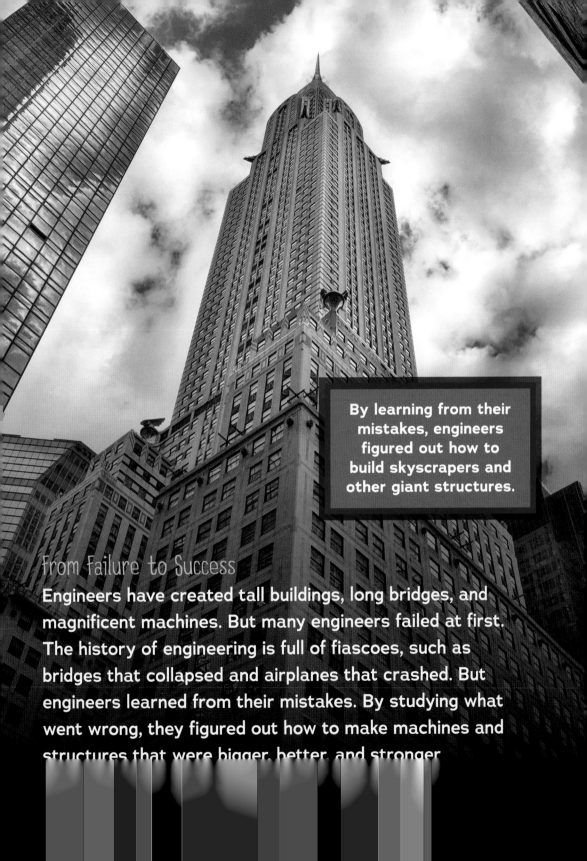

By learning from their mistakes, engineers figured out how to build skyscrapers and other giant structures.

From Failure to Success

Engineers have created tall buildings, long bridges, and magnificent machines. But many engineers failed at first. The history of engineering is full of fiascoes, such as bridges that collapsed and airplanes that crashed. But engineers learned from their mistakes. By studying what went wrong, they figured out how to make machines and structures that were bigger, better, and stronger.

Chapter 2

BUILDING BRIDGES

In 1867, leaders in New York City hired engineer John Roebling to build the Brooklyn Bridge. The bridge would cross the East River and connect the districts of Manhattan and Brooklyn.

Work on the bridge began in 1869. Disaster struck almost immediately. At the construction site, a boat crashed into Roebling's foot. The wound became infected and Roebling died. Roebling's son Washington took over the project.

John Roebling designed the Brooklyn Bridge, but he died after an accident at the construction site.

Building the Brooklyn Bridge was dangerous. Some workers walked on cables hundreds of feet in the air. Others worked in caissons under the water.

To build the bridge, workers sank caissons into the water. These giant chambers sat at the bottom of the river. Inside the caissons, workers dug sand, soil, and muck out of the river bottom. Working inside the caissons was dangerous. Some workers got caisson disease, caused by changes in air pressure. They suffered headaches, joint pain, and heart problems.

A Family Affair

Washington Roebling got caisson disease too. He got so sick that he could no longer work outdoors. Then another family member stepped in. Washington Roebling's wife, Emily, had never studied engineering. But she had learned much from her father-in-law and husband about bridge building. For the next eleven years, she helped her husband supervise the project.

Emily Roebling helped her husband supervise bridge construction.

WHEN THE BROOKLYN BRIDGE OPENED IN 1883, IT WAS THE LONGEST SUSPENSION BRIDGE IN THE WORLD.

The Brooklyn Bridge opened in 1883. At the time, it was the longest suspension bridge in the world. But at least twenty-seven workers had died from falls, machinery crashes, and other accidents during bridge construction. After the bridge opened, New York State passed laws to protect workers at dangerous construction sites.

Galloping Gertie

In the 1930s, engineers designed the Tacoma Narrows Bridge. This suspension bridge would cross Puget Sound in Washington State. One of the engineers, Theodore Condron, thought the bridge was too long and narrow. He warned that it would sway from side to side. The other engineers ignored Condron's warning.

But Condron was right. When the bridge opened in May 1940, it swayed and bounced. Workers nicknamed it Galloping Gertie. To fix the problem, engineers used steel cables to secure the bridge. But that didn't fix the bounce.

Cars drove across the Tacoma Narrows Bridge, even though it bounced and swayed.

Six months after it opened, the Tacoma Narrows Bridge collapsed into the water.

Travelers still used Galloping Gertie. They walked and drove across it, even though it bounced. On November 7, 1940, strong winds blew across Puget Sound. The bridge twisted in the wind. Frightened drivers and pedestrians hurried off the bridge. Eventually, the bridge broke apart and collapsed.

One life was lost: Before the bridge fell, a reporter drove across it with his dog, Tubby. As the bridge started to fall, the reporter escaped on foot. Tubby and the car fell into the water.

IN THE TWENTY-FIRST CENTURY, ABOUT NINETY THOUSAND CARS DRIVE OVER THE TACOMA NARROWS BRIDGE EVERY DAY.

After the disaster, engineers studied the problem. They figured out how to make suspension bridges more stable. The new Tacoma Narrows Bridge opened in 1950. It did not bounce or sway.

Failing Upward

In 1844, a gun exploded aboard a warship called the USS *Princeton*. The explosion killed eight people, including several top US officials. Swedish engineer John Ericsson and US Navy captain Robert Stockton had designed the ship and its guns together. But Stockton blamed Ericsson for the explosion. Some military leaders lost respect for Ericsson.

Ericsson designed another warship called the *Monitor*. It was made of iron. Unlike a wooden ship, the *Monitor* could withstand exploding shells and cannonballs. During the Civil War (1861–1865), the *Monitor* fought against another iron ship, the *Merrimack*. The battle proved the strength of iron ships in wartime.

Ericsson built more warships. People respected him again and called him a hero for his military contributions.

Chapter 3

SNOW JOB

In late 1979, workers in Minneapolis, Minnesota, began building the Hubert H. Humphrey Metrodome. Baseball and football teams would play there. The domed roof had two layers. The top layer was fiberglass. Beneath that was a layer of strong fabric. The dome was inflatable: machines pumped in air to inflate it, just like pumping air into a beach ball or inner tube.

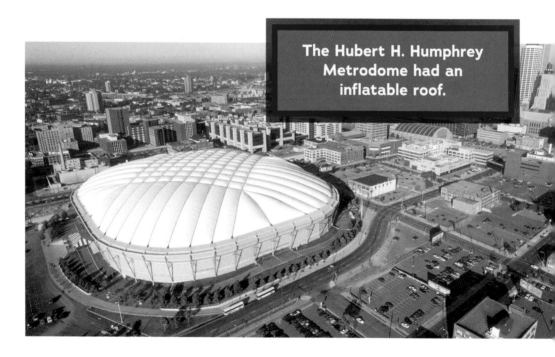

The Hubert H. Humphrey Metrodome had an inflatable roof.

Engineers mistakenly thought that the Metrodome could withstand snowy Minnesota winters.

Minnesota is cold and snowy. In 1981, before the Metrodome opened, heavy snowfall ripped a hole in the domed roof. Air from inside the stadium rushed out through the hole. The dome deflated.

Snow ripped the roof again in 1982 and 1983. In 1986, strong winds made more holes in the dome. Each time, the dome collapsed. Then workers repaired the damaged dome and reinflated the roof.

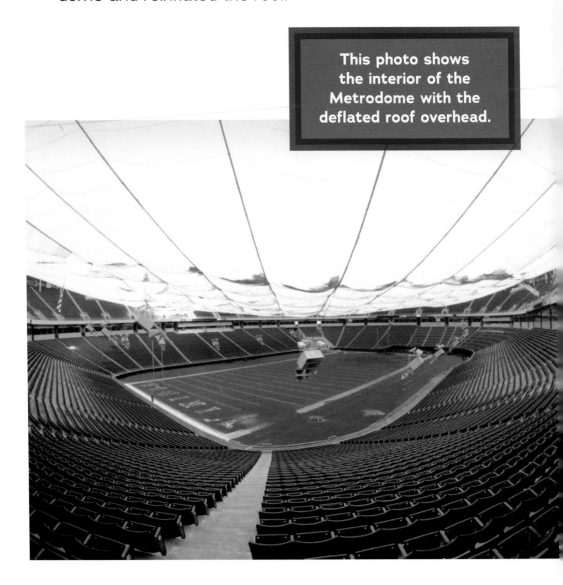

This photo shows the interior of the Metrodome with the deflated roof overhead.

Snow covers the football field
inside the Metrodome after a
roof collapse in 2010.

In 2010, during another snowy winter, 17 inches (43 cm)
of snow fell on the dome in one day. The dome tore and
collapsed again. Tons of snow fell through the damaged
dome and onto the stadium floor. Again, workers repaired
the dome and reinflated it.

THE ROOF OF US BANK STADIUM IS MADE OF STRONG PLASTIC AND STEEL. IT IS BUILT TO WITHSTAND HEAVY SNOWFALL AND ALSO LET IN LIGHT.

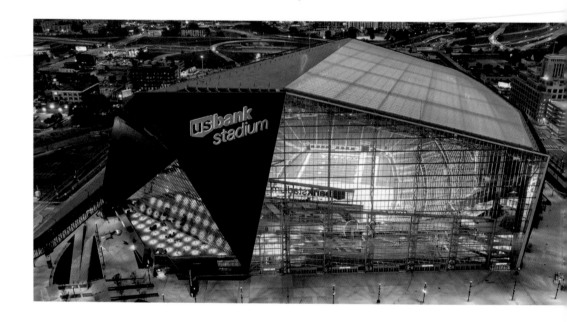

Repairing the dome was costly. Leaders in Minnesota decided to build a better sports stadium on the site. In 2013, work crews tore down the Metrodome. Workers built US Bank Stadium. It opened in 2016.

The new stadium roof is not inflatable. It is strong enough to withstand heavy snowfall.

The Road to Failure

In the early twentieth century, William Mulholland headed the Los Angeles Water Department. He oversaw building of the Los Angeles Aqueduct. This system carried water from the Owens River, in eastern California, to Los Angeles. Farmers in the Owens River valley were angry. The aqueduct took away water they needed to grow crops.

In March 1928, Mulholland inspected the St. Francis Dam, part of the aqueduct system. The dam leaked, but Mulholland said it was safe. The next day, the dam collapsed. A 78-foot-tall (24 m) wave of water rushed through the broken dam. The water killed more than four hundred people. Mulholland had ignored the danger when he checked the dam. He resigned from his job.

Although Mulholland was responsible for the tragedy, people still admire him as a leader of Los Angeles. The city has named roads, schools, and other structures in his honor.

Chapter 4

LOST AT SEA

Titanic, a British ship, made its first sea voyage on April 10, 1912. It was the world's largest passenger ship. It carried about twenty-two hundred travelers. It headed from England to New York City.

The company that built the ship said it was unsinkable. Its steel hull contained sixteen compartments. Even if two of those compartments were flooded, the ship would still stay afloat.

Titanic leaves Great Britain on April 10, 1912.

THIS CUTAWAY ILLUSTRATION SHOWS *TITANIC*'S LOWER DECKS AND INTERIOR STRUCTURES.

▼

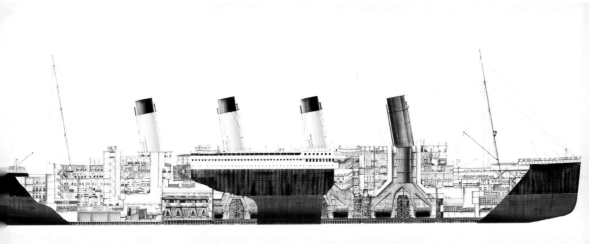

As the ship sped across the Atlantic Ocean on the night of April 14, it struck an iceberg. The iceberg hit some of the rivets that held the hull together. The rivets broke, and parts of the hull split apart. Water flooded into six of the hull's sixteen compartments.

The iceberg in this photo, taken near the wreck of *Titanic*, might have been the one that hit the ship.

As water rushed into the hull, the ship tilted forward and to one side. Because the ship tilted, water began flooding over the bulkheads. These walls separated the hull's compartments. As the ship tilted farther and farther, more bulkheads flooded. The ship began to sink.

Women and Children First

Some passengers got into lifeboats. But the ship had only about half the lifeboats it needed. Sailors loaded women and children into the lifeboats first. Then passengers realized that the ship didn't have enough lifeboats for everyone. Many began to panic.

A German artist made this painting of the sinking of *Titanic*.

A LIFEBOAT CARRYING *TITANIC* SURVIVORS NEARS A RESCUE SHIP.

▼

As the front of the ship sank, the rear of the ship rose out of the water. Then the ship broke in two and sank to the sea bottom. More than fifteen hundred passengers and crew members died. Some drowned. Others died of hypothermia in the freezing cold water.

After the tragedy, shipbuilding companies improved their safety practices. The company that built *Titanic* added an extra layer of steel to the hulls of its ships. It also added taller bulkheads to keep water from spilling over their tops.

Many nations joined together to create new safety rules for passenger ships. These rules included a requirement that ships carry enough lifeboats for everyone.

Modern-day passenger ships carry enough lifeboats for everyone and conduct lifeboat drills for crew members.

Glossary

air pressure: the weight of air around Earth or another body pressing down on the ground

aqueduct: a human-made channel or series of channels for carrying water from one place to another

caisson: an airtight and watertight chamber used for working underground or underwater

deflate: to lose firmness due to the escape of air or another gas

dome: a structure shaped like an upside-down bowl, often used as a roof

engineer: a person trained to design buildings, bridges, roads, vehicles, and other structures and machines

hull: the main watertight shell of a boat or ship

hypothermia: a condition in which a person's body temperature becomes abnormally low

pedestrian: someone who travels on foot

propeller: a device with a central hub and spinning blades, used to move a ship or aircraft forward

rivet: a large bolt used to fasten metal plates together

suspension bridge: a bridge in which the roadway hangs from steel cables supported by two high towers

Learn More about Engineering Fails

Books

Farndon, John. *Stickmen's Guide to Engineering*. Minneapolis: Hungry Tomato, 2019.
 How do engineers design bridges and buildings that are strong and safe? Using colorful illustrations, this book explains many engineering concepts.

Finger, Brad. *13 Bridges Children Should Know*. New York: Prestel, 2015.
 Discover how engineers designed and constructed the world's most famous bridges.

Slader, Erik, and Ben Thompson. *The Wright Brothers: Nose-Diving into History*. New York: Roaring Brook, 2018.
 Find out how Wilbur and Orville repeatedly tried to build a successful airplane.

Websites

Building Big
 https://www.pbs.org/wgbh/buildingbig/index.html
 Learn about bridges, dams, tunnels, and skyscrapers.

Engineering, Go for It
 http://www.egfi-k12.org/index_noflash.php
 This American Society for Engineering Education website introduces kids to the field of engineering. It includes fun facts and profiles of mechanical, aerospace, computer, and other kinds of engineers.

STEM and Engineering for Kids
 https://www.sciencekiddo.com/engineering-for-kids/
 Make engineering projects with everyday materials, such as drinking straws, hard candy, paper, and Lego pieces.

Index

Photo Acknowledgments

Image credits: Science & Society Picture Library/Getty Images, p. 4; Roger Viollet/Getty Images, p. 5; Library of Congress, pp. 6, 7, 14, 15; AFP/Getty Images, p. 8; mshch/Getty Images, p. 9; Oxford Science Archive/Print Collector/Getty Images, p. 10; Photo12/UIG/Getty Images, p. 11; Everett Collection Inc/Alamy Stock Photo, p. 12; Hulton Archive/Getty Images, p. 13; Comstock/Getty Images, p. 18; Todd Strand/Independent Picture Service, p. 19; Bettmann/Getty Images, p. 20; AP Photo/The Star Tribune/David Joles, p. 21; Gian Lorenzo Ferretti Photography/Getty Images, p. 22; Wikimedia Commons (PD), p. 24; De Agostini Picture Library/Getty Images, p. 25; Universal History Archive/UIG/Getty Images, p. 26; Everett Historical/Shutterstock.com, p. 27; National Archives, p. 28; landbysea/Getty Images, p. 29.

Cover: Rolls Press/Popperfoto/Getty Images.